Ulga Vulture's Makeover

Written by Colleen Jensen

Illustrated by Leslie Bascom

It is impossible to be invisible when you're a vulture.
But Ulga wished she was invisible today.

The Kookaburra brothers were playing
wing-tag around her and singing:

Kookaburras sit in the Old Quill School,
Looking at the new bird; she's not cool.

Laugh, Kookaburras
Laugh, Kookaburras
Ulga, you're a fool!

Ulga squeezed her eyes shut,
ruffled her feathers, and clamped her beak tight.

She couldn't stop the squawk that erupted from her gullet.

It stopped the entire lunch room mid-munch.
Squawkward!

SQUAWK!

Ulga started to cry. Not a real dainty cry –
more of a hiccupy, sniffly, snorting kind of cry.

Her wings heaved up and down in uneven jolts
and her red-rimmed eyes got even redder.

The other birds took to twittering
and tweeting about what to do.

Who would be brave
enough to help?

They knew it shouldn't be hard
– but Ulga was different.

The Flamingo twins, Candy and Mauve, jumped up,
waving pink hankies
and flocking to Ulga's rescue.

"Make way, make way," they said.

"With just a few tweaks, you'll knock those naughty birds over with a pinfeather" said Candy.

"I have the perfect shade of pink dye for your feathers in my hand bag."

"A few minutes in the bird bath will do wonders for you, Sweetie" Mauve added.

When the trio returned, Candy and Mauve raved over Ulga's exotic plumage.

Ulga stretched out her left wing,

stretched out her right wing,

shook her head and rolled her eyes.

"I need my carrion" she said.

"Luggage?" the twins asked.

"No – my lunch," Ulga huffed.

A gaggle of birds swooped around her.

Dan Toucan lectured her
on the benefits of fresh
fruits and seeds

instead of 'that meat substance'
she was currently eating.

Suzanne Pelican recommended
that she swallow her food
instead of shredding it –

'it's so much more appetizing.'

Nellie Quail offered her a sprinkle of grit for her gizzard –

'to help with digestion.'

This was too much for Ulga.

She started to choke.

Regal Eagle swaggered over
and gave her a mighty whack on the back.

"Thanks," she sputtered..

"It's what I do," Regal said.

"Here's a little jazz for your new image."

"Okay. Great. Thanks again," Ulga said

Next, a tap on her knee set off her reflexes.

"AAACCCKKK!!" Mallory Duck gasped as she skittered across the floor.

"Sorry!" Ulga hollered.

Good grief! Can this day get any worse?

"Ah Hem," Mallory cleared her throat.

"What now?" Ulga asked.

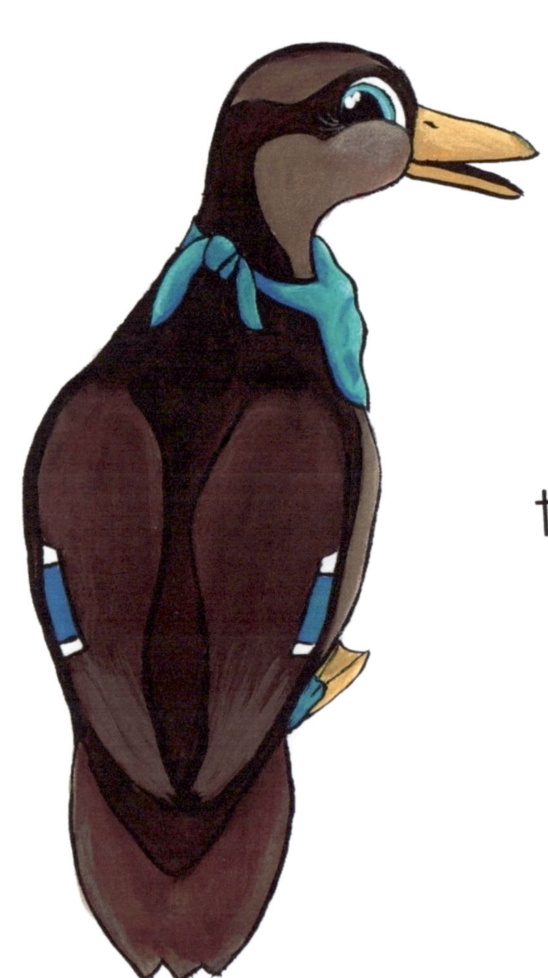

"Girl, you've got
to learn to move
that body like a Cadillac –

not a pickup truck,"
Mallory squabbled.

"Up, up! Shake it off.
Now, wings back,
tail feathers out,
head held high,
and strut, strut, strut. And glide."

Ulga tried to steer her bird legs in the same direction but crumpled into the splits.

She was ready to melt into the floor.

Ulga hung her head and migrated to the preening room.

Rue Cockatoo glanced up
from combing her crest

"Nice beak"

she said on her way out.

Really? Ulga thought.

It is big- and powerful. So are my wings.

It was time for Ulga
to look deep down inside her vulture soul.

"I'm Ulga LouJean Vulture.

I like stinky meat
and flying in circles.

I have wrinkly skin –
like my whole family.

I'm proud to be a vulture!

What's wrong with just being me?"

"Not a thing, Darlin'!" Candy said.

"Ya know, pink isn't your color after all. It'll wash out soon enough, Sugar," Mauve added.

"I wouldn't mind having pink claws," Ulga said.

"We still need to work on that walk," Mallory piped up.

"Okay, but you have to learn my one-of-a-kind Vulture Victory Dance," Ulga smiled.
"Bring it on," said Mallory.

It proved to be very catchy!

Bird Terms Glossary
(in order of appearance)

Pinfeather: a feather not fully developed
Exotic: strikingly, excitingly or mysteriously different or unusual
Plumage: the feathers of a bird
Carrion: dead and putrefying flesh
Gaggle: a group lacking organization
Swooped: a single concentrated and quickly effective effort
Grit: a hard, sharp granule of sand
Gizzard: a thickened part of the digestive tract
Preening: to groom with the bill or beak

First Edition
ISBN-978-1-5323-9842-1